The

Book of

HULGA

Wisconsin Poetry Series

Ronald Wallace, *Series Editor*

The
Book of
HULGA

Rita Mae Reese

ILLUSTRATIONS BY
Julie Franki

The University of Wisconsin Press

Publication of this volume has been made possible, in part,
through support from the Brittingham Fund.

The University of Wisconsin Press
1930 Monroe Street, 3rd Floor
Madison, Wisconsin 53711-2059
uwpress.wisc.edu

3 Henrietta Street, Covent Garden
London WC2E 8LU, United Kingdom
eurospanbookstore.com

Printed in the United States of America

Library of Congress Cataloging-in-Publication Data

Names: Reese, Rita Mae, author. | Franki, Julie, illustrator.
Title: The book of Hulga / Rita Mae Reese; illustrations by Julie Franki.
Other titles: Wisconsin poetry series.
Description: Madison, Wisconsin: The University of Wisconsin Press, [2016] |
©2016 | Series: Wisconsin poetry series
Identifiers: LCCN 2015036816 | ISBN 9780299308148 (pbk.: alk. paper)
Subjects: LCSH: O'Connor, Flannery—Characters—Poetry.
Classification: LCC PS3618.E4424 A6 2016 | DDC 811/.6—dc23 LC record available at http://lccn.
loc.gov/2015036816

this book is dedicated to

Betty Hester

1923–1998

If I were to live long enough and develop as an artist to the proper extent, I would like to write a comic novel about a woman—and what is more comical and terrible than the angular intellectual proud woman approaching God inch by inch with ground teeth?

Flannery O'Connor

Contents

3

Interlude
The Case of the Missing Virgin

4

5

6

Acknowledgments

My deepest gratitude to all of those who helped this book along the way. I hope you know who you are and how much your support, advice, criticism, and friendship have meant to me over the years. In the interest of keeping the acknowledgments shorter than the book, I will name only a few. I remain grateful for the support of the Rona Jaffe Foundation, whose gift came at a critical time in my life. I'm particularly grateful to the National Endowment for the Humanities for their Reconsidering Flannery O'Connor Summer Institute, where I met generous and inspiring O'Connor scholars. I'm also indebted to Arthur F. Kinney for his book *Flannery O'Connor's Library: Resources of Being* and Sally Fitzgerald for her heroic effort in collecting O'Connor's letters into *Habit of Being*, without which this book would not have been possible. I am grateful to the Harold Matson Co. and the Mary Flannery O'Connor Charitable Trust for allowing use of some of O'Connor's published and unpublished material. Thanks also to Marshall Bruce Gentry, who spearheaded the institute and welcomed my inquiries with remarkable graciousness. Very special thanks to my poetry group—Cynthia Marie Hoffman, Jesse Lee Kercheval, Angela Voras-Hills, Nancy Reddy, and Rebecca Dunham—who have rescued Hulga and me over and over again, to Nick Lantz for correcting my steering early on, to Maria Hummel and Kimberly Elkins for their keen eyes and even keener hearts, to Brandy T. Wilson for a thousand things, to Elizabeth for everything, and to Julie Franki for creating the illustrations that brought Hulga to life. And finally, thanks to Ron Wallace, who is a bright light among poets and men.

"The Grandmother's Sonnet," "Hazel Motes's Sonnet," "The Misfit's Sonnet," "The Lame Shall Enter First," "With Regina at Lourdes," "Learning to Pray. Again," and "Isn't" appeared as "Flannery's Crown" in *Alaska Quarterly Review*; "The Given Lines," "Revising History," "The Reward," "Displaced," "The Life You Save," "*The margin is for the Holy Ghost*," and "Everything That Rises" appeared as "The Given Lines" in *Alligator Juniper*; "Interior of Hay Loft, Day" and "Because She Wanted" appeared in *Blast Furnace*; "Flannery, Are You Grieving?" appeared in *Cortland Review*; "Exegesis: *The Tempest*" appeared in *Cream City Review*; "How to Lose a Leg" and "What Her Mother Knew When She Heard" appeared in *Driftless Review*; "Milledgeville," "Manley Pointer's Sonnet," "The Misfit's Sonnet," "The Lame Shall Enter First," "With Regina at Lourdes," "Learning to Pray. Again," and "Moral Error Theory" also appeared in *The Flannery O'Connor Review*; "Milledgeville," "Manley Pointer's Sonnet," "Your Body Is a Temple of the Holy Ghost," "J-O-B," "*There's wood enough within*," and "A Bird Sanctuary" appeared as "*The margin is for the Holy Ghost*" in *jubilat*; "At 36, Hulga Speaks of Love" appeared in *The Lavender Review*; "In Which She Reads the *Humorous Tales* of Edgar Allan Poe" appeared in *Quiddity*; "On the Problems of Empathy" appeared in *Rattle*; "Feast Day" appeared in *The Rumpus*; "Welcome to Milledgeville" and "Hulga as Sara in *The Book of Tobit* Who, Possessed of a Demon, Was Given Seven Husbands and Killed Each on Their Wedding Nights" appeared in *Verse Wisconsin*.

Her heart,
never still,
digs its
red hole,
forcing roots
into the absence.

Feast Day

When we eat wheat   we devour the sun
    so in this room filled with permanent flowers,
let us celebrate not with fasting
    but with Red Sammy Butts barbecue.
Lord, let us sink to our knees under the weight
    of our Southern appetites. Let us devour
    cornbread & turnip greens, rum balls & goose eggs
    brined in the salt of resurrection.
Let us fill our hollow legs with pink chiffon pie
    & Cokes spiked with coffee.
Let us devour the landscape—
    every damn cotton field in Georgia
& beyond, every real & imagined plantation,
    every pig farm & waiting room.
May we eat & eat & eat   Lord,
    & make no end of this, her hunger.

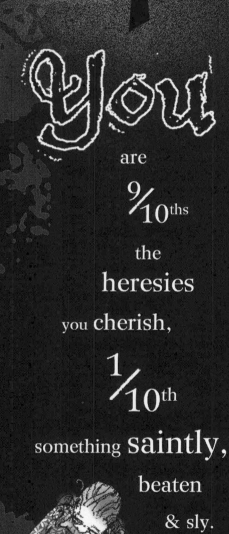

1

you

are

9/10ths

the

heresies

you **cherish,**

1/10th

something **saintly,**

beaten

& sly.

The Given Lines

beginning and ending with lines from Simone Weil

There is the nothingness from which we flee
& the nothingness toward which we go.
Hell is nothing, God is nothing   & we
are the nothing lost between. Out of our pain

we make countries, maps, direction. She
has made herself into a map of the Red Forest
where an albino swallow circles & drops,
where boars & bison & roses

have made an almost home—but no human
ever comes   & none ever will.
All of the empty spaces have the outline
of someone missing.

Her heart, never still, digs its red hole,
forcing roots   into the absence.

Revising History

To be rooted in the absence of a definite place,
to belong to mountains that have been removed,
to valleys that have been filled—a world gone flat—
is to learn geography as affliction. To be rooted

as if my spine extends invisibly down
into dirt & rock, deeper than drills can go,
tethered to some hot core, is to lose part of myself
when I leave. Nothing thrives here

& I can't thrive anywhere else. We
don't get to choose which part of ourselves
we'll lose, or even to know what it is we've lost.
We don't get to know where we should go

or how to hold still or any of the other things
Pavlov's dogs & other martyrs must know.

The Reward

Pavlov's dogs & other martyrs know
after great pain   a bell rings.
Their eyes strain to see the vial sutured
in the cheek below   catching

drool they know   is worthless,
or worse.   After being made fluent
in Russian pain they become his   & deathless,
or close.   A bell rings & the heart relents

until everything sounds like a bell.
The vials fill   with faith in master
& reward—   it is all
they can offer the reward that is master,

but even this holds a drop of alchemy in its dregs—
a lesson in giving   in the spirit of one who begs.

J-O-B

Learning to give in the spirit of one who begs
means first you have to learn how to beg.
I think of my drunk friend telling
a homeless guy in DC: get a J-O-B.
A few years later, drunk again, hits a tree.
He told me once that his father would
come home drunk, come into his room
with a gun, threaten to blow his brains out.

He never said if he'd pretend to be asleep, cry,
plead, pray or how he'd rise the next day,
go to school, return to that room, lie down & wait.
Never said if he knew why any man
would want to see his own son begging for his life.
The stories about miracles confuse everything.

With Regina at Lourdes

The stories about miracles confuse everything.
Your mother still believes in them
as if they are pebbles she is following out
of the forest. Her faith stands still while she
waits for another one to drop from the blue sky.
You make your own path, stump along on it
while the wolf inside you is tearing
the place apart—out, God. Let it out.

When the airfare is booked for Lourdes,
you protest but go. Love is to mortality
as cure is to disease & all of them
are killing you. In line for the baths,
you are lost again in the hell that is your body
until her pain for you opens the door

The margin is for the Holy Ghost

The pain that opens the door   is not God
though you worship it   & fear it
    & pray to it with your loose, odd
devotion, your stuttering, cross-eyed faith. Were it

only a little taller   a little less full
in the hips   it wouldn't stun the nuns
to silence   burn the priests to fulminate
on redness & virginity—the sun

you carry low, the woe you carry high.
You are 9/10ths the heresies you cherish
1/10th something saintly, beaten & sly.
On your face love lies garish.

You turn off the lights when you look in the mirror
& pray   there's a usage for every kind of error.

Isn't

There's a purpose for every kind of error
until there isn't. Everything has a use
or there is a landfill with a fire
always burning and this is Hell, or it isn't.
(*Always* a bur in your shoe. Hundreds
of years, thousands, yes, but *always?*)
There is a black dog licking its paw until
it bleeds, until teeth scrape bone.
There is a girl, a girl like fire afraid
there's nothing left to burn. There is
a panther behind bars 100 years & beyond
the bars, a nothingness draining the world.

You are mostly empty space—a nothingness
from which you flee & toward which you go.

2 **F**irst you must enter the **woods**. **No**, the woods must enter **YOU.**

How to Lose a Leg

First you must enter the woods.   No, the woods must enter you.   So
      stand very still and think of something else.
This is easier if you are a girl, an only child, lonely.   If
      your head is in books, in the clouds, in clouds of books.   If you
are, right now, thinking about King Midas.   Not the goldfinger of Midas
but the donkey ears.   And not King Midas really but his barber.   Not
the barber taking off the king's hat   but the barber digging a hole
      and shouting into it   *King Midas has donkey ears!*
About the itch of those words in your throat.   Inside the pockets
of your father's field jacket   your hands cup two dead quails.
      Despite the birds   you must not think
about guns.   You are not sentimental about birds   or death
      —this is why he brings you.   Don't think about birds
or him,   think only about Midas, about donkey ears. Then
the loudest shot you've ever heard.   It is the sound
of the ground opening beneath you.   It is
the birds and the trees and the air

                              shouting you down into the hole.

What Her Mother Knew
When She Heard

That she is a three-legged beast
with two weak hearts

That the dogs are now wolves
the birds all crows
the girls are all sticks
and the boys all stones

Welcome to Milledgeville

the soul
    is a bird sanctuary
        the way Milledgeville
    is a bird sanctuary

—

a young boy sits
    in the lone movie house
        of the soul

a pretty girl
    turns cartwheels
        on the lawns of the soul
    until she sinks through the surface of the earth

a woman
    shoots her husband
        in the servants' quarters of the soul

—

sometimes all you can hear
    is the beating of wings

Hulga's Fairy Tales

You've never liked
        Red Riding Hood,
most of all
        because your mother
            is already a wolf,
especially when sleeping.
        Nothing could induce you
            to go to her narrow bed
when you were a child,
        convinced she'd leap up
            with her big eyes
& big white teeth
        & swallow you whole.

All children know, or should,
the sudden turns love can take.

On the Problems of Empathy

1

Twice a year the orphans come.
Like Job's children, pawns in a bet
made with the Devil.

2

You and your mother watch
from the porch as Father Whiskey's car
rolls up the long dirt drive.
The orphans inside ignore the fields,
the cows, the pond, the patch of woods.

3

When you were younger,
you begged for a brother,
or even a sister.

4

What should you say to an orphan?
You think of your mother's prelude to sympathy:
"There's nothing easier
than burying other people's children, *but . . .*"

The orphans are beyond sympathy.

5

Sympathy being one of the problems.
How far does it go?
Not quite to the horizon.
Not even to the trees beyond the pond.

6

The orphans, their still-breathing,
lye- and cabbage-smelling bodies,
are also a problem.

7

Father Whiskey with his lazy eye
thinks a good Catholic family
with only one child is both
problem and solution.

8

One blue eye looks at your mother.

The other looks at God
looking at you.

9

You know sympathy requires action
or at least words, and that empathy is merely
the crippled gravity we each emit.

10

Father Whiskey sees God looking at you as if
—if you believed in the Creed, the Holy Ghost,
and all that he has tried to tell you, if
you could even look a statue
of Mary in the eye—
then you could reach out a hand,
lay it on this boy's scrubbed forehead,
make him your brother.

11

Later, in college, in a winter of mind and place,
you will read Edith Stein's
On the Problem of Empathy.

Now though she is of no help to you.

12

You stand on the front porch
and wait for the miracle
to begin in your shoulder
and travel down through your fingertips,
the way you've heard lightning
tries to escape the body.

13

In a few months there will be different orphans.
Then the time comes but no orphans.

14

Years later, in a city where you can't speak
the language, you will pass a woman
sitting on the pavement, a burnt-out shell
of a woman holding an infant. The baby is sleeping,
on his head a robin's-egg-blue bonnet, spotless.

15

Your problem is you feel too much, or not at all.

16

Their grown bodies move past you.

In Which She Reads
the *Humorous Tales* of Edgar Allan Poe

Fifteen years old. Her father's home from Atlanta, not for the weekend but for good and not home really, but back at Regina's sister's. He can barely walk and he's so tired. She's advanced from *The Book of Knowledge* to the *Humorous Tales* of E. A. Poe. When she's not reading she keeps it beneath her bed. In his dim room alone with him, she tells her father the stories.

The Spectacles

She skips the part about his mother and grandmothers marrying at fourteen, fifteen, sixteen. She describes how handsome the man is and how vain, how he can't see well but refuses to wear glasses and so ends up marrying his own great-grandmother. She can feel her father smile, try to laugh. She knows she should go. She musn't wear him out, Regina says. Even in the dim light she can see his face is redder than ever and rough with scabs. She presses her lips against a still-smooth patch on his forehead. Outside his room she realizes she forgot to tell him the ending.

The System of Dr. Tarr and Professor Fether

Alone in the afternoon he argues with debts he cannot pay. His skin is peeling in strips, as if it were wallpaper in a too-damp room. The doctor comes and goes and nothing gets better. She slips inside his room. She imitates each of the lunatics at the dinner table who think they are chickens and champagne bottles. They had been humored in their madness until they rebelled, tarring and feathering their keepers.

The Man That Was Used Up

Weep, weep, my eyes, dissolve. Half my life has sent the other half to the tomb but her father is not dead, not yet, he is in his room and she's locked out. She slips her father notes under the door and waits for an answer. She needs to tell him how the story about the General is known by everyone but this man. How finally, after asking everywhere, the man arrives in the General's room and finds a strange-looking bundle on the floor; he kicks it and it begins speaking to him and then bit by bit—hair, arms, eyes, teeth—becomes a man again. After his funeral and for the rest of her life, when she thinks about the story, she remembers the General going to his room alone and removing parts of himself one by one. And there is always a room, and always a man inside coming apart.

First Dream

A house was on fire. Freud smoking beside my bed. He woke me. I dressed myself quickly. Mother wanted to try to put the fire out. Where will we live? Where will we live? she wept. With your dreams you burn down every home I've ever found.

Phenomenology of Sow

Future means only you are no longer gilt,
    means boars shoving your body into
endless farrowing. Means piglets always
        at your teats and boars behind.

    The only pleasure food
but no relief from appetite
    until the thick chain
and the hired man's dark hands with his long knife

and a bucket to catch the blood.

The girl gets the rat poison from the shed
    and the sow rouses herself to eat.
Within minutes a large invisible hand
        shakes the sow's swollen body.

The white froth on the mud might form
    a constellation
    but the girl cannot make it out.

By afternoon the stillness

draws Shot to it, his knife
opens the sow's belly,
his mind a tightening circle
of *maybe   just maybe.*

A grown man on his knees
   in mud and blood, shaking.
  Her eyes open and dry.

For nearly twenty years Shot's tears
   germinate inside of her,

grow into appetite, desire,
   fill her body with twisted roots
   and branches. No way to weed anything out.

The slick piglet slips from his grasp.
    The girl watches.
Not a weed, but something God planted.

Exegesis: *The Tempest*

Her father gone 272 days. She
    attends parties, church, class.
    People's faces all around her
      moving around food and words,
    and her mother's face refusing
      to cave to grief,
while she is a ship full of men

    near to drowning.
      While she is a ship breaking apart.
      While she is Miranda on the shore
shouting *Father! Father! Father!*
    Don't drown the men that is me.

Mostly she is in her room
    dressed in his old shirts.
      More and more she is Caliban
      alone while the normal girls get
their shipwrecked nobles
    delivered to their shores.

Her mother in the doorway
    with a new green dress,
      a perky Miranda from town,
    another chore.
There's wood enough within,
    Hulga answers.
    (*Woods*, she amends.)

Hulga as Sara in *The Book of Tobit* Who, Possessed of a Demon, Was Given Seven Husbands and Killed Each on Their Wedding Nights

In the mirror is not a beautiful woman.

Hulga looks for Hulga elsewhere.   Hulgaheart stumbles,

    falls, picks Hulga up, stumbles. It is the picking up

which is the worst.   *Stay down*, Hulgaheart hisses

    but Hulga wants up   *up*. Wouldn't it be easier to marry?

to stay down?   *Yes!* Hulgaheart says.

    Yes! Hulga's family says. Hulga puts on the dress

and swims through the mud of the smiling day.

    But on the night's shore, the question is waiting:

Does he love Thee   for thyself   alone?

    Hulgaheart is a bloody bird in a saint's hand,

a bat caught in Groom's hair   a knife

    they tried and tried to keep away.

Milledgeville

is the nothingness from which she flees
& the nothingness toward which she goes.
Is the frozen world of Parmenides
where she was raised & where she was returned,

where existence is uniform & unchanging,
where just down the road is the state asylum
where bad children are sent, where she
could still be sent if she's not careful,

where half of her *was* sent—her inner Hulga,
bloody fist knocking on sleeping doors.
To avoid the bloody fist she stays at her desk,
writing letters to friends who left home

& stayed gone, who thrive on the leash of exile
in the absence of any definite place.

Hazel Motes's Sonnet

To be rooted in the absence of a definite place,
is to find only a half-busted chifferobe
when you go home. Home just a house
that'd fall over if you lean on it. The town,

if that's what it was, withered up and slunk away
like an old dog who knows he'll never be fed again.
Home after some sort of war (what sort
you still don't know, don't care now that

it's spit you out). What you need is a few nights,
as many as are left, in a friendly bed,
something to eat that wouldn't nobody
call rations, something in your head

other than what you've been told, other than what
Pavlov's dogs & the other martyrs already know.

Your Body Is a Temple
of the Holy Ghost

Pavlov's dogs & other martyrs know
that consciousness is only a mirror
the body created to look at itself,
that each body is only a body

like all other bodies, mortal in every cell,
asking *who is the finest?* Know some spells
are never broken. The body a mirror too,
and between the mirrors a dollhouse

miniature of infinities. They know this world
is a wind of reflections tacking between
unlandable shores. Ask, *who among us*
isn't haunted by a reflection in search

of a mirror? A reflection determined to teach
each of us to give in the spirit of one who must beg.

The Lame Shall Enter First

Everything here is given in the spirit of begging.
Hulga, 19, at the drive-in movie theater flea market
drifting among tables carefully arranged
with Matchbox cars, doilies, kitchen utensils,
car tires (with rims) stacked in solemn
but cheerful black columns. Behind each
intricate taxonomy is a hard-used human body
with eyes that light on Hulga & move on.

O theater of matchbox ambitions, you have
reconstituted Eden with doilies & kitchen utensils!
The three-story screen above the scene
a billboard for silence—
                                    as blank as God.
The stories about miracles confuse everything.

The Life You Save

The stories about miracles confuse everything.
All of the drunks & sleeping babies
unscratched in car wrecks & how friends
swore you were better off without a seat belt

because then you could be thrown clear—
how much we believed driving home drunk
& free may not have made us safer
but if we made it home alive proved

God loved us more. Today give me a sign,
one that even I can read, telling me
how to get back to the before-dead, how to rise up
in still-sweet flesh, how to believe

there's an unnumb heaven waiting for us
& that this pain is going to open the door.

A Bird Sanctuary

The pain that opens the door
sometimes opens windows too.
You lie on the floor as if
you're floating on a sea of board.

You watch the birds fly in. All you want
is for them to pick you clean.
Instead they make nests, lay eggs,
raise their feathered young. You pluck

out your hair, one by one. Blind fingers find
each loose thread and pull. You pick
yourself clean. The floor is cool and smooth,
the air fills with flight patterns

and something like happiness in between:
a purpose for every kind of error.

Moral Error Theory

There's a use for every error, a use
for the loudspeaker of the car dealership
a half mile up the road that intrudes
into this circle of trees, into these acres
of house & pond & barn you once
called home, a use for the voice that says
call on line three but that means
any categorically imperative element
is objectively valid, which means
there is no right or wrong,
there's just a loudspeaker inside your chest
like a giant funnel siphoning away
the pond, the barn, the trees
into the nothingness from which you flee.

Hulga

believes in Hell.

Her bed

a place to pray

& a house of corrections.

The Red Clay Virgin

The men say Hulga carries
a temple between her legs
& no one worships there.
Heresies echo off the damp walls
all night—

other suns, other worlds,
lost apostles, new revelations.
Hulga can smell the Holy Ghost,
hear Jesus, taste God.

The women say Hulga is an anathema
both in Greek   & in Hebrew:
Hulga is set aside for God   & Hulga
is banished, exiled, forbidden.

Hulga says Hulga believes in Hell. Her bed
a place to pray & a house of corrections.
One guard, one prisoner,
one cell   —all Hulga.

The Vanishing Point

Mostly school was questions seeding her skin
like buckshot—no, like tiny vanishing points.
Her philosophy professor's final question
follows her home:
Is there—at most—one empty world?

If he were on the train with her,
she could point out a dozen or so.

There was a question of what you get
when you divide zero by infinity.
There was an example using potatoes.

The train has its own philosophy,
the rails another. She is not well. It feels
as if her blood is a train moving
in the wrong direction. She contemplates Providence.
She contemplates Edith Stein dropping notes
from a cattle car through towns where people
might remember her,
on her way to becoming one of millions
of vanishing points, converging
into an invisible star.

If a train leaves Iowa City at 9 a.m.
and travels 50 miles per hour,
and Zeno boards midway,

how long will it take to die?
The potatoes rot and grow
while the errors accumulate.

As the train approaches the event horizon
it gets longer and longer.

Is Hulga divided by God
Hulga or God?

Inside she gets impossibly small.
Outside, scraps of paper blow by.

Hide & Seek

O Lord, you create darkness, & it is night

& her love is night,
   is summer girls outside
   while inside bride & groom
     sleep in stiff dominion
You have never been able to love
   what you were supposed to love

When she closes her eyes & counts,
   aren't you careful
   not to hide too well? You can no longer
     bear the pain of not being found

One night she comes to your hard bed,
   your wooden leg
and says *Listen*
   to the animals creeping forth,
   seeking their meat from God

Immaculate

Hulga puts on her dead father's clothes and becomes a man.
When he grows tired of walking the acres of his kingdom
or just short of breath, he sits at his desk and writes.

What happens is *The Case of the Missing Virgin*.* Every morning
he goes to the *Virgin* to see what happens next.
As always with virgins, nothing happens except everything.

There is a crime and a petulant thirst for justice.
There is secrets, lies, confessions. There is sinners, there is hands,
there is angry God. There is a thing with wings that bothers people.

There's blood. There is a thirst for something other than justice.
There is plot thick as Regina's Irish stew. We now know
the *Virgin* is his only friend. Pity that she's dead.

*There are several theories about the origin of *The Case of the Missing Virgin*, with many scholars claiming that Hulga's father wrote it before his death and she simply discovered the manuscript and then presented it as her own. The Immaculate School believes that his clothes wrote it. The flannel of the shirt held the story until it dripped and then ran from the ends of her fingers. After Hulga's death, her mother burned the clothes as well as many of Hulga's papers.

At 36, Hulga Speaks of Love

In wine is truth and in rum freedom,
    the freedom to get up from the porch
  with her mother still talking.
In rum is the Judge in her room,
    sitting beside the books behind glass.
  Love should be full of anger, he intones,
    and she nods, sits on the bed, takes off her shoes.
Judge weighs evidence against Hulga day and night,
    mostly night.

Love, she repeats, but behind her absent gaze
    at the saint in the corner
  she is *parting a pink gold shower of hair,*
    dividing it upon a back bare its length.
  She had thought she was all done with asking
but in rum is (God help her) the consent to love.

In rum also is a radio playing
    so far away she can't make out the tune,
  a shadow of sound slipping toward Hulga
    through years and hundreds of miles
  from the girl in the apartment downstairs.
This the only music she listens to.

She is *bending to kiss exactly the hollow of her back,*
    exactly the spot

best suited to receive first [her] lips
and then [her] cheek.
Love, and *do* what you like, he mutters. Hulga is
multiplied by the dozens of women
she has never seduced. She is cast into a legion of swine
sailing over a cliff.   And she is flying.

Immaculate Rejections

Dear Mr. (a small pleasure), *We read your submission with interest but regret to say it does not fit our catalog at this time.*

No morning more quiet. The *Virgin* is beneath the letter.
Back but further away, burrowing down into Hulga,
twisting where she can't reach, like a child wrapping
itself around a parent's legs. She sends it out again and again.
No one can recognize her genius. This makes her happy,
is the surest sign of genius she'll ever have.

Mailbox at the end of the long dirt drive thrums,
a magnet of emptiness.

Then a plain envelope in the box, no note about a package.
She's in such a panic she opens the letter
standing in the driveway. Her only copy.
She sees flames, she sees trashcans, she sees pages
blowing along some busy street, under strangers' feet.
She reads the letter several times before the words take root:

They want her.   *Virgin* won't be coming home.

Second Dream

A house was on fire. Joy was beside my bed. / She woke me & made me stand. We faced each other. I realized / I was naked & so was she. I had a scalpel / in my hand. She closed her eyes. There was a voice / coming from nowhere but filling the room. It said *cut her open*. She kept her eyes closed. Though I didn't want to my hand moved & inserted the scalpel just below the navel & pulled up / like zipping a coat. When the scalpel reached her ribs her eyes opened, my eyes opened   the blade / going through my ribs my throat my dearGodyes / my tongue

4

Hulga is a block of hay

beneath the SNOW.

If an angel comes,

she does not know.

Casting Call for *Temps Mort*

Someone should make a movie out of Hulga, its only scene:
    Hulga in the hayloft, its setting: the absence
        of the bible salesman,
            the absence of everyone

& Christopher Walken playing Hulga
    lying there, with one leg gone—
        the absence of his dancing
            the absence of his flying,

or Philip Seymour Hoffman, not *Hunger Games*-Hoffman
    or even *Boogie Nights* but *Happiness*-Hoffman
        sweating up there in the hay,
            his face rewinding itself to the Big Bang

    as the air empties of everything but Hulga.

Oh God, what we need is a faster time machine and deliberate death.
    We need 1986 & Warhol directing

& you & I sitting for hours, for days
    watching Hulga lie there all alone,
        us in our first apartment
            with Sinead O'Connor

& Virginia Woolf at 17 on the walls,
    & inside our little cable-less television

Hulga played by Jane Fonda, by Candy Darling,
    by Joe Dallesandro with his headband on,

by Valerie Solanas with her bad aim. One after the other of them,
    & you & I on the couch, in our bed, in the kitchen
        our bony hillbilly hips & lips transmuted by its glow,
            which is only the absence of anything blocking the light.

Interior of Hayloft, Day

She is a block of hay, like
    Sleeping Beauty in reverse,
like Waking Ugly, she has taken
    gold and spun it into straw.

She has time to remember
    while her mother searches,
makes frantic phone calls,
    calls *Joy! Joy!* and finally *Hulga*

which makes Hulga want to run
    and put a finger to those thin lips,
makes her forget that she cannot run
    or stand or even speak

because she is too busy remembering
    the tale of Sleeping Beauty
and despite the sounds that reach her now
    she believes the farm is all asleep,

all under a curse that fell
    like a light snow.
She has time to remember the story
    wasn't Sleeping Beauty at all

but Rumpelstiltskin, with the miller's daughter
    caught between her father's bragging

and some strange man's desire for
    a living being to call his own—

the poor girl   little more
    than a pretty womb.

Hulga is a block of hay beneath snow.
If an angel comes, she does not know.

After Hours of Staring Out
at the Pond

After hours of staring out at the pond she sees God
is a mirror that retains the reflection
of anyone who has ever looked into it.
Hours of staring don't keep darkness from coming.
Dark is the pond flooding the world.

Because She Wanted

Because she wanted to be closer
to God she took off all of her clothes.
She unnamed them as they came off
God like water all over the drowning
Over and over and over God
but under too deep under everything
stays under except God+ God. One nation
under Hulga. Nation like a fist
in the small of her back
That was years ago is how now felt then
Now covering her body at last.

Mrs. Freeman Knows the Signs

She doubts
the girl even knows
the facts of life
(she tried
explaining them
to her once.
Better off,
she'd thought then,
her not knowing).
Birds and bees
all buzzing
around Hulga's head,
which is quiet
and empty now,
as if her brain sank
down to her stomach
where it is growing
into a child.
Sweet Jesus.

Birth

The doctor says a cyst
   Little sister at last, tardy friend
   or stubborn brother afraid of Mother
   burrowed now into the wrong body

   No matter   You will think of names,
   only names

Surgery approaches like a train
   Lie beneath it, perfectly still
A mask is placed over your face:
   Breathe the gas that floats you up
It is all darkness
Up is dark and down is dark
   Do not be afraid
   See the lights
   the tops of heads
   and the body
   centering it all
The body is yours, or was
Inside that body another darkness

You cannot close your eyes
because your eyes are closed
   See the surgeon's gloved hand,
   see the scalpel like a light,
   showing you what they all see—

a sexless fist of teeth and hair
nameless inside you

See the surgeon lift
this prehistoric self,
place it in a metal pan
Watch the nurse cover it with a blue towel

Emptiness rises up, covers the world

Post-op

After that, years pass
    or maybe a week.
Hulga stubbornly worships growth
    & so the child grows.
There are two lives to live now.
      One, anyone can see.
      The other is his & hers alone.
She names him
    & then repents of it.
He needs no name.
I-am-that-I-am,
    everything else an admission of failure,

even the name you give yourself
    just a box to bury you in.
Together, they are that they are,
    not were or ever will be.

The Grandmother's Sonnet

There is the nothingness from which you would flee
& the nothingness toward which you go.
There is a secret room in a house in Tennessee
that you fill with antebellum silver
& your own beauty that flashed so quick
no one saw. You fill it with a good husband
& you the necessary wife & mother.
In this room all of your patience decays.
Every step you take is directed toward that room,
every step another detour until suddenly you
arrive at the door & there's nothing—not even
a room. There never was a house in Tennessee.

No matter where you turn, here you stay,
rooted to this absence in Tennessee.

Manley Pointer's Sonnet

To be rooted in the absence of a definite place,
to be not from any place, just from near someplace,
is to carry always with you this portable altar
to the brokenness everyone tries to hide.

To know this world is held together only
with tape & glue & clumsy stitches,
is to be driven from door to door selling snake's ink.
Is to be the loneliest boy in the lonely world,

the last emperor of clarity.
The altar grows heavier at each house—
all those glass eyes & wooden legs.
No one is ever glad to see you

so when you go you leave them knowing
everything Pavlov's dogs & other martyrs know.

The Misfit's Sonnet

What Pavlov's dogs & other martyrs know
is all some people's ever fit to learn.
Obedience never was my cup of tea, or coffee.
Listen, nobody came along
to raise my daddy after he passed.
I sat up and watched & he ain't never moved
all that night. I put my hands on him & said *rise!*
Rise rise rise, you sonafabitch.
Nothing, just Mama crying in the corner,
begging me to stop. So I left & kept leaving.
That's me there on the side of the road.
You think you've done gone past, don't you?

When I'm done with you, you're gonna know
how to give like you're begging.

Displaced

Learn to give in the spirit   of one who begs.
Outside the grocery store, a man is begging.
We are broke & I have always been poor.
Though you have no job, you roll down your window.

I won't let you give & all the way home
we argue. I point out we don't know what he's done
or will do. He might have beat his wife, raped someone,
who knows? & if we gave, he'd just get drunk.

His life hopeless either way.
Years later, he's probably dead & I've lost track of you.
Still, I can't give—I just let each one take until
she gets tired of taking & leaves. Everywhere

I see the cast on his arm & the black dog at his feet.
Stories about miracles confuse everything.

There's wood enough within

The stories about miracles confuse everything:
You awake to the wolf of Gubbio licking your hand,
St. Francis bringing you breakfast in bed.
Your room is the lion's den & you are Daniel.
Your room is a whale & you are Jonah,
Pinocchio, Ahab. The windows disappear,
the walls lean in. The walls of Jericho may fall
but not these walls. These walls are trees
& you are where someone loves you best
of all, your room is the woods & you
are only a girl, but a whole girl, a girl
without pain, standing still at the edge.

Then comes a knock like a flame catching the trees, & you,
poor wooden girl caught, as pain opens the door.

Learning to Pray.
Again

The pain that opens doors is the closest thing
to a miracle you'll allow. You never wanted
to be a saint though you could've been
a martyr if they killed you quick enough.

Your death's not quick. The wolf devours
you patiently. You listen to the gnawing
on bone and to doors closing again inside
of you. The wolf always on the wrong side,

as if your body is a trap he got caught in, a trap
growing smaller. You & he both know the world
is made up not of atoms & molecules
but of hinged pain. You've opened every door

save one. Behind that door stands God
& a purpose for each of our errors.

Everything That Rises

There is a purpose for every kind of error
& you're still asking what yours will be.
It is one of your weaknesses that you believe
someone or something can spin you into gold.

The black dog at the foot of the bed stirs,
digs a hole to bury you. Nothing to do
but lie still, taste dirt. Nothing will save you
from tragedy except comedy, which is worse.

Let the ground find a use for your body
which was my home, which was never my home.
Let your words sink beneath your tongue
which was my root.

Close your eyes now & let the nothingness
from which you flee be the nothingness

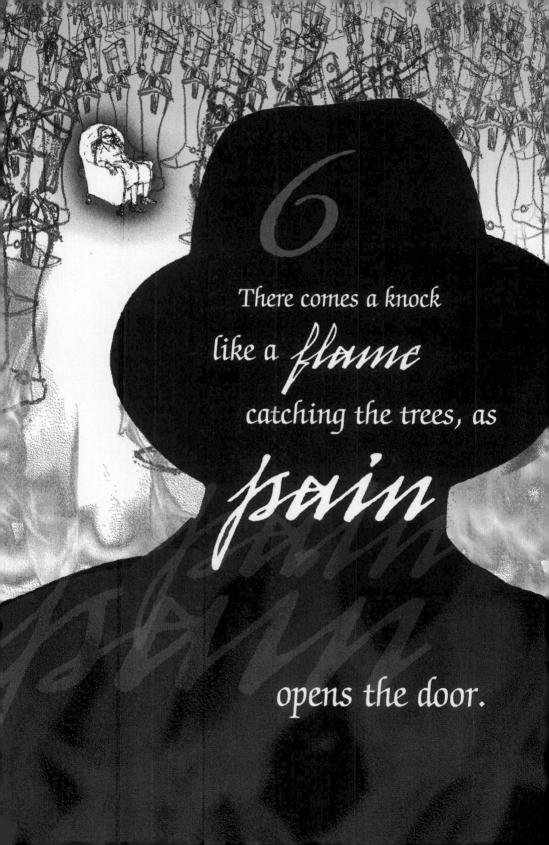

6

There comes a knock
like a *flame*
catching the trees, as

pain

opens the door.

After Flannery's Death,
Regina Cleans Her Room

The words on all those pages, the words in all those books

little flames whispering to each other planning a conflagration

a conspiracy of flames & the house on fire

the house on fire & Joy beside her bed

the house is fire & fire is Joy & Joy is fire burning the house

Flannery O'Connor's Peacocks
Go to Heaven after She Dies

I intend to stand firm and let the peacocks multiply, for I am sure that, in the end, the last word will be theirs.

Flannery O'Connor

Her mother shipped them out, no longer having to tolerate the way they ate her flowers, or picked them, or sat on them. One pair went to a cancer treatment center run by nuns but the peacocks didn't cure anything and their sharp cries would force patients from sleep. The peacock never reminded them of immortality through Christ or if it did, this thought unnerved them. The strutting, preening, hollow arrogance was too much to associate with heaven—not here, not now. The next pair went to a monastery where the monks were trying to run a retreat. Guests wanted quiet, which the monks were but the peacocks were not. Perhaps in Flannery's mind monks and peacocks were like good cops and bad cops for Jesus. The eyes of the Church, the black orbs nestled in iridescent chenille that the peacock would fan out, were not what the guests wanted to see. One monk defended them but a new monsignor found a man in Ohio who would let them strut and scream on his land, safely away from the paying guests. In Ohio, the peacocks and the farmer lived, neither one troubled by the other's violent dreams.

Pieta with Regina

As if grief could be made graceful,
    as if her death finally arriving
  could give you back a mother's arms.

To hold the only body you have ever cradled

the body you have forgotten how to cradle
     and now must bury.

The body that will not rise. Though the sound
    of her one foot hitting the floor
  is embedded in mornings—or is just the echo—
then the long pause before the dragging of feet.

You live in that pause. You are worn out
    from listening,
     from not looking
    to the doorway where you do not believe
you will see her body but
    cannot believe you won't.
  No matter how you hold your arms.

Flannery, Are You Grieving?

With the wolf's teeth sunk firmly
in your organs, his jaws working
at your heart all night long,
you stop to read Hopkins:
Margaret, are you grieving
Over Goldengrove unleaving?

You drag the typewriter to the hospital
and proudly report that the doctor
says that though you can't work *you can write fiction.*
You take the pages of "Parker's Back"
and write the final revisions by hand.
Leaves, like the things of man, you
With your fresh thoughts care for, can you?

You write brief notes to friends,
send the story to Betty in lieu
of a letter. Your eyes are nearly swollen shut.
Ah! as the heart grows older
It will come to such sights colder.

You said the tumor had to go
or you did. And now you know
it was both. Alone in your room,
you might have been able to laugh
at that thought—just once.

By and by, nor spare a sigh
Though worlds of wanwood leafmeal lie;

A man in a white suit is walking down the corridor
and you will be turned over to him.
You know he started walking toward you
the moment you were born. Your panic rises.
And yet you will weep and know why.
Now no matter, child, the name:
Sorrow's springs are the same.

Your kidneys fail and you slip into a coma.
Nor mouth had, no nor mind, expressed
What heart heard of, ghost guessed:

I read your last letter slowly,
67 exhausted words
from Tarfunk to Raybat.
I am sunk in a sorrow that lasts for days.
How many times will I turn to that last page?
Each time knowing as if for the first time:
It is the blight man was born for,
It is Margaret you mourn for.

Nothing can have a destination
which is not its origin.

—Simone Weil

Appendix: Quotes from Simone Weil

Nothing can have a destination which is not its origin. The contrary idea, the idea of progress—poison. The plant which bears such fruit should be torn up by the roots.

[In the form of wheat, we devour the sun, and, at the same time, the human spirit.]

The fullness of being is identical with nothingness for the purposes of abstract thought; but not so when one is fleeing nothingness and directing one's steps toward being. There is the nothingness from which we flee and the nothingness toward which we go.

To be rooted in the absence of a definite place.

Pavlov's dogs and martyrs in general.

It is not easy to give with the same humility that is appropriate for receiving. To give in the spirit of one who begs.

The stories about miracles confuse everything.

The pain that opens the door.

There is usage for every kind of error.

(T)hey are another human species, a compromise between a man and a corpse.

A very beautiful woman who looks at her reflection in the mirror can very well believe she is that. An ugly woman knows she is not that.

Notes

Hulga is a character from Flannery O'Connor's short story "Good Country People," in which a thirty-something woman with a wooden leg and a PhD in philosophy attempts to seduce a Bible salesman. I have used her as a lens through which to view the life of O'Connor and to examine the distance between an author and her work.

The book epigraph is from a letter published in *The Habit of Being*, © 1955 by Flannery O'Connor. Reprinted by permission of the Mary Flannery O'Connor Charitable Trust via Harold Matson Co., Inc. All rights reserved.

The three interlocking crowns of sonnets (see sections 1, 3, and 5) all utilize lines from *The Notebooks of Simone Weil* translated by Arthur Wills and *First & Last Notebooks* translated by Richard Rees. See the appendix for the full quotations Weil used in these poems and others.

"The margin is for the Holy Ghost" was Betty Hester's admonition to Flannery O'Connor, warning her not to write in the borrowed copy of *The Notebooks of Simone Weil*.

The quotation in "Hide & Seek" is Psalm 104:21 as paraphrased by Saint Jerome.

The quote "love should be full of anger" is from Saint Jerome, in a letter "Scolding a Monk for Having Abandoned the Desert," and appears in O'Connor's short story and unfinished novel "Why Do the Heathen Rage?" Italicized lines in "At 36, Hulga Speaks of Love" are taken from the unpublished drafts for that novel, held at the Flannery O'Connor Collection, Special Collections, Georgia College Library and Instructional Technology Center. The lines have been altered from the original to reflect a change from a male character to female. Text copyright © by Flannery O'Connor. Reprinted by permission of the Mary Flannery O'Connor Charitable Trust via Harold Matson Co., Inc. All rights reserved.

Temps mort literally translates as "dead moments." It is "a French phrase used to describe a manner of staging and filming that stresses long intervals between actions or lines of dialogue in which no major narrative development takes place" (Kristin Thompson and David Bordwell, eds., *Film History: An Introduction*, 3rd ed. [New York: McGraw-Hill Higher Education, 2010]).

"There's wood enough within" is the first line Caliban speaks in Shakespeare's *The Tempest*.

The epigraph to "Flannery O'Connor's Peacocks Go to Heaven after She Dies" is from the essay "Living with Peacocks"/"King of the Birds," © 1961 by Flannery O'Connor. Reprinted by permission of the Mary Flannery O'Connor Charitable Trust via Harold Matson Co., Inc. All rights reserved.

Italicized lines in "Flannery, Are You Grieving?" are from "Spring and Fall: To a Young Child" by Gerard Manley Hopkins.

For additional notes and suggested reading, please visit http://ritamaereese .com/books/notes-on-the-nothingness/.

Wisconsin Poetry Series

Ronald Wallace, *Series Editor*

(B) = Winner of the Brittingham Prize in Poetry

(FP) = Winner of the Felix Pollak Prize in Poetry

(4L) = Winner of the Four Lakes Prize in Poetry